Travis Jordan, in *Connection*  glimpse into an educational landscape we should not just admire, but one that we should as a profession, indeed as a nation, aspire to reach and inhabit. Travis is at once disarmingly vulnerable in describing his own educational journey, and profoundly wise in offering prescriptions to heal hurting children, and to humanize over-standardized and teacher-centered classrooms. Heart and soul, he's committed to the simple aspiration to make classrooms, schools, and the world a better place through daring to care, to reach out, and to put faith in the power of relationships. This is an important and inspiring read about the author's journey, and our own, to become better humans – and ultimately, better educators. One comes away from reading the book aspiring to be both. – DAVID FLOWERS, PH.D., retired English teacher, coach, administrator, and superintendent; promoting innovations that make school more engaging, student-centered and aligned with the rapidly changing world to which our children are heir

Rarely does a book have the authenticity that Travis Jordan brings in *Connection over Conformity*. Travis leads with his heart in the workplace and in this book as he shares about the importance of relationships, passion, and purpose in every school. His stories, both tragic and triumphant, will challenge you and inspire you. Together we can make education stronger and more meaningful for every student. – DAVID GEURIN, award-winning principal and speaker; author of *Future Driven*

Travis Jordan writes from the heart in this thought-provoking book. He provides you with a commonsense approach to reaching all students through fostering relationships. This book is a must read for all involved in education. *Connection Over Conformity* will make you smile and touch your heart, but most importantly, it will ignite your passion see positive change in education. – STACY MURSCHEL, principal

Travis Jordan affirms the importance of professions in education and the difficulty of the immense emotional labor that comes with the work. Through Travis's vulnerable account of his and others' experiences and struggles, he reminds us that the only true silver bullet in education is connection. This book will reignite your passion, call forth your purpose, and inspire you to challenge any system that prioritizes our children's data ahead of our children's dreams. Amid a youth mental health epidemic, the timing of this book is perfect. – AMY FAST, assistant principal; author of *It's the Mission, Not the Mandates: Defining the Purpose of Public Education*

Connection over Conformity is a must-read for educators as we grapple with the importance of helping kids form positive connections and manage their emotions. It's a journey into the realities of being a student, a teacher, a leader, and a human being. It's a call to action to inspire and be inspired by others. – DR. NICK POLYAK, superintendent; co-author of *The Unlearning Leader: Leading for Tomorrow's Schools Today* and *Student Voice: From Invisible to Invaluable*; connect via Twitter: @npolyak

In *Connection over Conformity* Travis Jordan gets to the heart of what education is about: people, relationships, and building a school community that has a constant focus on doing what's best for kids. You can feel the passion Travis has for education as it radiates from the pages as you read! – ADAM WELCOME, educator, principal, keynote speaker, and ed week blogger; NSBA 20 To Watch; co-author of *Kids Deserve It*; author of *Run Like a Pirate*

In his book *Connection over Conformity*, Travis Jordan lays his heart out for us to learn from. It's an excellent read for anyone in the field of education. – TODD NELSONEY, White House Champion of Change; 2018 John C. Maxwell Transformational Leadership Top 10 Finalist; NSBA 20 to Watch; CDE Top 40 Innovators in Education; TEDx Speaker; connect via Twitter: @TechNinjaTodd, #KidsDeserveIt, #TellYourStory, #SparksInTheDark

Travis Jordan is a leader with passion, purpose, pride, power, professionalism, and persuasion. In *Connection over Conformity*, Jordan, a school superintendent, father, and husband, shares a blueprint for humanity in educational leadership. By sharing the experiences of himself and others, he shows the reader how humility and humanity in leadership are the keys to preparing the next generation of learners and leaders. The current educational obsession with testing and sorting is challenged in Jordan's well-written and powerfully persuasive book about the real needs of our nation's youth. Connection Over Conformity is a wakeup call for us all! – MICHAEL LUBELFELD, author and superintendent

connection

over conformity:

a pathway to success that travels through the heart

TRAVIS JORDAN

Travis Jordan
Beulah, ND 58523

TJordan.org

Connection over Conformity: A Pathway to Success that Travels through the Heart / Travis Jordan – 1st Edition

ISBN 9781099023538

Dedication

I'd be nothing without my family. This book is dedicated to my wife, Jennifer Jordan, and our four children, Tayten, Jeter, Brinley, and Madden. These people mean everything to me and have supported and encouraged me through this endeavor from beginning to end.

I dedicate this to my parents Agatha Bernhardt and Steve Jordan. I might be biased, but I have amazing parents.

This book is also dedicated to my siblings Andrew and Brandon. I wouldn't be who I am today without them.

Finally, I dedicate this book to the family of Cassidy Andel. Cassidy's life on earth was way too short, but in her death, she gave me a passion to change the world.

"A lot of people have gone further than they thought they could because somebody else thought they could."

– Zig Ziglar

CONTENTS

FOREWORD

I've never done this before. I have never written a book. I take that back: I've written two books in their entirety and thrown them both away without sending them to the publisher. Honestly, I'm insecure. Who would want to read a book written by me? I live in rural North Dakota and work at a school surrounded by prairie. The closest metropolis, Bismarck-Mandan, is an hour and fifteen minutes southeast. I have no accolades other than that I was the Wilton Miners' boys basketball MVP in '99. I'm pretty sure I'm the only one who even remembers that. I scored a 21 on my ACT. Who could I possibly inspire?

The jury is still out on that, but my passion trumped my insecurity – so here I am anyway. I've come to realize that we shouldn't neglect our passions. When we do that, we begin to eliminate our purpose. I continue to ask God what my purpose is and eventually I return to my passion and my computer, pouring out words that demand to be spoken. I can't ignore the fire that's burned inside me for years, so I don't care if my wife and mother are the only two people who read this. But if you're reading this and you're *not* my wife or my mother, you may catch me patting myself on the back. And if you haven't been forced to read this book or found it in your hands by mistake – you might catch a double-pat.

This book encompasses many aspects of life but centers around the needs of our world's number one asset – children. I'm a school superintendent, and I need to call attention to a shift that's imperative if we are to steward children's education well. This shift, which cannot happen solely within the walls of the school, requires a renewed mindset – a change in the default setting of our vision. As we strive to meet the complex needs of this nation's children, we must stop seeing with our eyes alone and begin seeing with our hearts.

I hope this book gives you hope. I hope my passion ignites your passion. I hope my purpose gives you purpose. I challenge you to allow your heart to be your eyes – even when everything in you wants to cling to the status quo. And since this journey isn't meant to be done alone, feel free to tweet your thoughts to @Supt_Jordan along way.

While you're flipping to the next page, I'll pat myself on the back one more time because you've read this far and you are, indeed, flipping to the next page.

CHAPTER 1

A Heart's Reflection

What we see with our eyes can blind us from reality,

but our hearts can perceive the truth.

CASSIDY

I remember it like yesterday. I was in the second month of my new position as a school administrator. The day was no different than any other day. The foot traffic in and out of my office was consistent with days prior. Sometime in the middle of the afternoon, Cassidy came to visit me. I knew her well. As a sophomore, she was involved in many aspects of school. In fact, I'd just written her a letter of recommendation to supplement her application for president of our local chapter of Family, Career, and Community Leaders of America (FCCLA).

I could tell she was distraught the minute she walked in, and I quizzed her about what was bothering her. Cassidy eventually gathered the courage to tell me she was being picked on. Despite my guidance and empathy, she refused to give me names or specific examples – so I connected her with the school counselor, reminded her that my door was always open, and sent her on her way.

Fast-forward to that evening. My family and I were spending the first night in our new house when we heard a knock on our door. It was Cassidy. She was crying. She told me she was ready to share names and specifics on the negative behavior she was facing. I was conflicted about how to respond. My conscience told me to invite Cassidy in – but my education preparation won out. I asked her to come by my office first thing in the morning to get it all straightened out. As she walked away, I wondered if I'd done the right thing. I went to bed worried but ready to help Cassidy in the morning.

As I got ready for work the next day, the phone rang. It was my superintendent. Moments earlier, Cassidy had taken her own life.

Tears started flowing as I dropped to my knees. I couldn't stop crying. Her family lived just across the street from mine, and I'll never forget the agonized screams I heard from her house as I got in my truck and headed for school. The pain and sorrow that engulfed her family shot directly across the street and into my heart. I cried all the way to work; when I got there, I shut my office door and continued to cry. My heart was aching for her family and friends, and my mind was in a million different places. Could I have done something to prevent this? Should I have invited her in? Did I miss an opportunity to help a child?

Unfortunately, many students can relate to Cassidy's distress. Hundreds of thousands of children that are suffering in our schools. The statistics on mental illness, neglect, and abuse are utterly staggering, and many of these students wear happy-go-lucky attitudes to school just to survive. I recommend you do your own research on these numbers, because they're important – but the purpose of this book isn't to provide you with a litany of statistics. Instead, I ask you to allow your heart to bear witness to the following three stories.[1] Let's start with Mandy.

MANDY

Living with anxiety makes life a bit more interesting. Doing even the simplest things can cause the most thought and worry.

---

[1] Names (except my own story), dates, and places have been changed to respect the privacy of these individuals. Stories have been minimally edited for clarity and grammar.

When I was in the eighth grade my whole class had to attend a medical camp and anything medical used to be the only thing that caused my anxiety . . . until this camp. At one of the stations, I passed out in front of my whole class. It was honestly embarrassing and when we left everyone kept laughing at me and asking me these ridiculous questions about it. For some days after this experience, I didn't go to school because I was making myself sick by all of the anxious thoughts I was having.

After the medical camp my whole world changed. I was constantly worrying about every little thing and it was out of control. I was not the same person I used to be. I was short tempered with my family to the point where they were scared to talk to me. I almost was unable to do anything. One day I was driving home from my grandparents' house with my dad when I started having a horrible anxiety attack. I had to quickly pull over and my dad had *to drive. For a while after that day I didn't drive, and I would not go in my dads' truck. I only had my permit at the time and driver's education class was coming up in a few months, so I needed to drive before I could take the class. I barely could drive half a block and started having another anxiety attack. After this happened my mom talked to me about going and seeing a psychologist.*

When I first started seeing the psychologist, I had to go to a city which is over an hour away once a week. My friends would ask me why I was gone every week and I just told them I went shopping because I didn't want them to know I needed help. I felt embarrassed or like I was weak for needing help from someone else. Going to therapy helped me only for a short time. I was better as long as I continued to go to my appointments. After a couple months they told me I was doing better and didn't need to come back. A few months later it started to get worse, so I had to start therapy again

– and a cycle of improvement and decline started. Today I am on anxiety medication and I still go to see my psychologist every few weeks. Even with the medication and therapy, life is not perfect. Nothing can never fully take away anxiety. I still deal with it with all the help I've gotten. The interesting thing is no one at school knows this is what I deal with on a daily basis. Throughout school and sports, I look as if I'm fine, but my mind is going insane and I'm overthinking all day long.

Playing volleyball was not easy with anxiety. When I started to get to the varsity level it was hard for me to forget about mistakes I made because I was scared of being taken out and what everyone in the crowd was saying about my mistakes. Once I made one mistake I thought and thought about it until all I did was make mistakes. When I would be subbed out of the game I sat on the bench and my only thoughts were, "I'm going to sit on the bench every game now and I will never play again." It was hard for me because all I wanted was to be a good hitter and I knew I had the potential, but it felt as if my mind was stopping me.

After volleyball games, practice, or a normal school day, I most look forward to going home and seeing my dog, Doke. I got Doke for Christmas in 2016. He is a golden retriever and I got him to help with my anxiety. Most people think dogs cannot help but he helps more than anything else. Whenever I've had a bad day and my thoughts are everywhere it's like he just knows. He will come lay by me on the couch and put his head right on my lap. I never tell people that Doke is supposed to be a therapy dog because the one time I did I was made fun of for it. It gave me more anxiety because it made me feel as if I was stupid. Right now, my biggest worry is attending college next year without my dog. Life will be harder not having him to come home to and to help me feel better. He really

has been my biggest therapy.

– Mandy

Mandy is a remarkable student. She's popular. She also has a hard time getting out of bed every day. Being vulnerable, honest, and integrated is a challenge for her. Many students look up to her, but many students don't truly see her. Her teachers don't truly see her. But she's worthy of being seen, accepted, celebrated, and loved. Every human being has that need, and that need doesn't shut off during school.

ZOEY

I was born in California 39 years ago. My mom died instantly in a car accident (both me and my dad were also in the car) when I was 18 months old. My dad had a few cuts and bruises; I broke my arm, leg, hip, and had to have reconstructive surgery on my face. That's how I got my beauty scars on my face. I was in a full

body cast and had to relearn how to walk after.

My dad was already messed up with drugs and alcohol and

I think this made it worse. He was a big time nationally syndicated

radio guy with a killer voice. By the time I was seven he became

abusive. He burnt bridge after bridge and wasted all his money on

drugs and alcohol. We didn't have a place to live at times! I

remember sleeping on the radio station floor for a while . . . until he

got fired . . . then his friends' floors . . . until we got kicked out. Then

we roomed with a lady and her daughter until my father couldn't

pay rent.

My dad dumpster dived for food at grocery stores, and we

ate food that the shelter gave us – like ketchup and rice, and corn

meal pancakes.

When my dad had nowhere else to turn in California, he turned to an old friend who owned a radio station in North Dakota. I was 10 when we moved here on Amtrak with two suitcases. My dad eventually sobered up and remarried – and I met my best friend here – but he stayed pretty messed up from his addictions and remained abusive.

I remember the day I fought back. I was 15 and he was yelling and screaming and hit me as I was holding a huge can of coffee grounds, which spilled all over when his blow landed. I powered up and hit my 6'6 father before locking myself in the bathroom with my back against the door and my feet against the toilet. Any respect I'd had for my dad was long gone.

At 17 I decided enough was enough and with the help of a friend and her dad, I entered the foster system. Tears rolled down my face that day I walked into my foster home because I was free but had also left the only family I had. Still, it turned out to be the best decision of my life. I didn't have any contact with my father again. He ended up going back to drugs and was found dead in his apartment right after I had my daughter.

I married my first love at 21 and my daughter was born at 22. That was the happiest day of my life. Becoming a mother changed me into a stronger person. I realized what an independent strong person I needed to be as a mom and what I really wanted in life. It didn't work out between my husband and I, but he was great to his little girl, which is all that mattered to me. I thought it would be best if we went our separate ways at the age of 28.

I finished up cosmetology school and at my first job, the man who would change my life walked in. The one who gives over and over again, gives every ounce of love that he possibly can, loves me unconditionally and doesn't care who knows it, and has taken my daughter in and loves her as if she was her own. We got married when I was 31.

Around that time, I was diagnosed with lupus and a blood clotting disorder, which made it harder for my second husband and I to get pregnant again. It took seven months of daily shots before we conceived. Our daughter was born at 35 weeks and 4.6 pounds – but she was only in the NICU for 10 days. I almost died having my baby girl, but we both made it – and despite her still-petite frame, she's the biggest sweetheart!

My eldest daughter's dad passed away when she was 12, but she's a fighter and I'm so proud of her. She is kind, funny, smart, sassy and we have a super close special bond.

So why tell you all of this? I want anyone and everyone to know that no matter what they have gone through or are going through, that's not how the story has to end! Get up, dust yourself off, become a little bit of a badass, work your butt off, be a good person, believe in yourself and do whatever it is that you want to do in life. Know that you deserve someone who loves you with all their heart and treats you well!

Today I'm living my best life with my two girls and wonderful husband. I own a daycare and am a network marketer who has been blessed with rapid professional growth. If I can do it, I'm pretty sure anyone can. Just be stubborn (I got that in the bag) and go conquer your dreams. You get to decide how the story ends.

– Zoey

Zoey, a friend of my wife, is a truly outstanding woman. She's doing remarkably well despite her upbringing. Her feats of healing are inspiring, but the trauma she faced crushes me every time I read it. And I'm crushed knowing that many children have similar stories. They're walking our school hallways with severe pain and trauma – and we're blind to it. It shouldn't be this way. For children to truly flourish, we must make our schools a safe space to express problems, confusion, frustration, fear, and passion. Academic expectations must come second to empathy, or we will fail to educate our children. We may even attend their funerals.

TRAVIS

This is my story. As a student, I carried the heavy burdens of fear, anxiety, and depression. Not many people knew this about me. In many ways I resembled a happy-go-lucky child. What presented externally wasn't indicative of my internal chaos – proof that the realities of depression and anxiety can be imperceptible to the body's eyes.

My family lived in Webster, ND for the first five years of my life. Webster is a town you'll miss if you blink when you pass by it. I attended kindergarten for a half year in Starkweather, just ten miles north of Webster. Halfway through my kindergarten year, my father accepted a job almost three hours away. We packed our things and moved to Wilton, ND – and the transition impacted me deeply.

I was never diagnosed, but I'm certain I developed separation-anxiety disorder as a result of this move. (At any rate, the internet tells me that's what I had – so it must be true. Right?) Mayo Clinic includes the following common symptoms of this disorder: "excessive distress about [. . .] being away from home or loved ones," "constant worry that something bad will happen [. . .] causing separation from parents or other loved ones," and "refusing to be away from home because of fear of separation" to the point of "significant distress in daily functioning." Separation from my parents was such a source of distress for me that my mother practically had to drag me into the school each day. Often, my teacher let me lay in front of the classroom door while I cried hysterically. Exhausted, I'd eventually fall asleep on the floor. I was terrified I'd never see my parents again after they dropped me off, and to cope, I'd get permission to go to the bathroom just to see if my brother's coat was still on the rack outside his classroom door. If it was there, I knew they hadn't left me.

As a result, I didn't do well in school. Frankly, I didn't care. I rushed through things. Once, my mother started a dime jar to motivate my school attendance (and a dime a day was a lot of money in the '80s!), but distress and detachment pervaded my educational experience. During the third grade, the school visited with my parents about putting me on an Individualized Education Plan (IEP). At the first IEP meeting, staff told my mother that I would never achieve more than a "C" average and that I had learning disabilities that might rule out college. I became a regular occupant of the special education classroom; various accommodations were made for me; "fixes" that were meant to motivate me failed to change my behavior or love me out of my fear. Anxiety had completely engulfed my mind.

I was on an IEP up until the end of my eighth-grade year. I had grown comfortable in the daily routine that had accompanied it. I was doing less work, getting help, and it got me out of the regular classroom. I was coasting through school and doing just enough to get by – but truthfully, I didn't need an IEP. When my mother told me the story of that first IEP meeting, everything changed, and I set out on a mission to prove my teachers wrong. Enough was enough.

As I engaged more academically, the separation anxiety started to fade – but something darker than the prospect of academic honors distracted me from a preoccupation with the potential loss of my parents. I was bullied regularly for two things: being skinny, and loving basketball. Every day, my body was criticized. My constant eating and iron pumping didn't make me look bigger or stronger in the eyes of my peers. My body was such an acceptable target that a group of upperclassmen encircled me one day and pushed me around like a pinball. Similar experiences were frequent, but I never reported them – perhaps because some adults were no better. I can still feel sting of tears in my eyes as my middle school health teacher told the class to look at my chicken legs. My teacher was unfazed by my reaction. To make matters worse, my passion for basketball trumped my opportunity for social status. I'd shoot baskets until my fingers bled while other kids partied and labeled me a "mamma's boy."

But my passion for basketball kept me going. It became my coping mechanism – a way to escape to a place a triumph. When I shot baskets, I could see myself playing in big games and making the final shot. And nobody could take the euphoria of those daydreams away from me. With a basketball in my hands, I was untouchable. Basketball was the drug that made feel immune to the persistent negativity around me.

The dark moments were vicious. Feelings of despair and helplessness rattled me; I often cried myself to sleep. Other nights, after attending my first funeral, a fear of spirits kept me awake or sleeping on the floor of a family member's room. I was torn between a plethora of fears. I didn't fully grasp that I was impressionable, that death is scary, that depression and anxiety can be neurological as well circumstantial. Without answers to my mounting questions – without a permanent sense of belonging or the ability to physically rest – I felt alone and a little crazy. But basketball gave me purpose, and my loving family gave me hope. I thank God every day for the gifts of love, family, and basketball.

Ultimately, I proved my teachers wrong. I became "book smart" and had moments of triumph even as I endured high school bullies. Two especially unforgettable moments came during my senior year. The first victory was basketball related. We'd just lost an away game and were boarding the bus to head home. My coach got on the bus and told me that somebody wanted to talk to me back in the school. I wasn't in the greatest mood, but I got off the bus to find out who it was. It was a college basketball coach; he offered me a scholarship to come and play basketball at his school. I will never forget the feeling of that moment. My hard work, dedication, and passion had paid off. I met my doubters with results. (Ironically enough, I chose not to play college basketball. And I'm going to leave that hanging here just in case I decide to write a second book.) The second victory was announced during my senior English class. The principal walked in to announce to our class who the salutatorian and valedictorian were. The salutatorian was announced first. It wasn't me, and I wasn't shocked. I *was* shocked when he announced me as the class valedictorian. I cannot even explain the joy I felt in that moment. For the second time, I had turned "you can't" into "I did." Both victories were announced in a moment, but they were long-fought and hard-won. Other victories have followed.

Today, I have a beautiful 10-year-old boy who is the spitting image of his father: skinny, unable to gain weight, scared of ghosts, extremely intelligent, and deeply passionate about sports. (Seriously – he can tell you the rosters and stats for just about every pro sports team.)

I also have a drive to make school a safe place for him and every other kid, and I'd like to propose a new performance-based curriculum that will program students to feel safe.

Not really. If you believed that for a second, you've missed everything I've shared up to this point. The data-driven solutions we implement to close achievement gaps often fail, as exhibited by continually low-performing schools and students. Data has value to the extent that it helps us identify patterns, but it's often biased and incomplete – so it doesn't guarantee an accurate picture – and it often fails to demonstrate causation. Furthermore, human behavior is a variable factor. To rely on data for student success and wellbeing is to rely on information that's incomplete at best and misleading at worst.

We know this, but it doesn't stop our data-driven approach to student success and educator evaluation. We align professional development based on inadequacies in instruction. We build professional learning communities that vertically and horizontally align our curriculum. We require No. 2 lead pencils and heavy, dark marks on tests while our students have heavy, dark bags under their eyes and spend their lunch hours in the locker rooms because they can't afford food. Why do we demand that children operate in an educational system that isn't set up to help educators see and properly respond to students' fears, obstacles, and passions?

Conformity to certain standards is highlighted and prioritized over the health of students. This is backwards. We can't expect students to learn at high levels if their minds and bodies are not functioning at high levels. A malnourished student will have difficulty concentrating. An anxious student may fidget and disrupt the class. A student fighting depression may feel like school doesn't even matter. It follows that we're sabotaging the learning process by not prioritizing students' social and emotional wellbeing. We collect and review data, learn new curriculum, attend professional development sessions, and implement accommodation after accommodation without incorporating holistic wellbeing into the structure of the typical school day. Suicide rates continue to rise.

Humbly, and with the authority of my personal experiences plus fourteen years as an educator, I'd like to submit that we as educators need to prioritize the whole student – and that communities and governments need to support this endeavor in every respect.

CHAPTER 2

Being Human

It's okay to feel.

THE KEY

I've established that we need to prioritize the whole student, rather than standardized student performance – and that healthy relationships are vital to the success of curriculum. It follows that being human (empathetic, considerate, humble, honest) is the foundation of healthy, authentic relationships.

A few years ago, a student walked into my office with extreme anxiety about semester tests and reluctance to take his anxiety medication because of the stigma that surrounds doing so.

My response could have been generic and vague: "Just take them; they'll help." Instead, the first words out of my mouth were, "I take anxiety medication, too." And then I told him I suffer from anxiety daily. He abandoned his shame when I was vulnerable and honest. Acting as a human being instead of a put-together role deisolated the student and helped him have realistic expectations of himself.

I CRIED

"I Cried" is a blog post I wrote and am sharing here, unedited, because it's another concrete example I have of simply being human.

Two days ago, I broke down. I was in my office and I had just gotten off the phone with an individual and it sent me over the edge. I started crying. I'm a superintendent. I'm not supposed to cry. I'm supposed to lead with conviction. I'm supposed to have strength and show this strength at all times. Crying is a sign of weakness. At least this is the perception right?

I think it's crap. Yesterday as I was crying. I closed my door, and I had a moment. I was stressed and overwhelmed with anxiety. I had had enough. I cried. I'm an adult. I'm a superintendent. I'm human.

I'm not telling you this for sympathy. I'm sharing this story so that maybe somebody out there can find hope in it. I'm sharing this story so that maybe someday we will realize that mental health issues in adults is just as real as mental health issues in students. I'm sharing this story because I want people to understand that it's ok to be human. To laugh, is to be human. To cry, is to be human. I don't care who you are or what your position is, it's ok to feel. You don't need to mask your feelings to show masculinity.

This moment came on the heels of one of my children telling me that he cannot wait to be an adult because life will be so much easier. To which in my mind I was saying "I hope that someday you have a child that acts just like you." Can't believe I even thought that, but the words we are told growing up somehow tend to be the words we use as grownups. Thanks mom and dad. If only my son knew though how uneasy life can be for adults too.

Listen; we have a mental health crisis in this world and we need to recognize it sooner rather than later. We live in a world of disconnection but yet the world has given us tools to make connection easier. We live in a world in which we allow distrust and hate to penetrate every aspect of our lives, and it often shows up before we see the positives. Many times we fail to see the positives altogether.

Schools across the country are faced with a lack of services and resources to help their students. Not to mention schools across the country are faced with many teachers suffering from mental illness. This is a full-blown crisis and part of the solution is pretty simple.

Connection. Connection is the answer. We all have the need to feel like we belong. We all have a need to feel like we matter. We all need that somebody that makes us feel like a someone. This takes little effort. This takes us to programming our minds to see the positive in every situation. This takes us putting trust before distrust and love before hate. This takes us abandoning the selfishness of our own minds to open up and discover someone else's. This takes us to use our ears more than our mouths.

I broke down. I'm okay. I do suffer from anxiety and I manage the best I can. I have many people in my life that have formed connections with me, and I with them. I'm lucky. But not

everyone is. As we approach the holidays make it your goal to

connect with someone. Make it your goal to make someone feel like

a somebody.

Don't be afraid to cry. Don't be ashamed to break down.

Great leaders are not fake leaders. Great leaders are human. Great

leaders make mistakes. Great leaders can cry.

I realize that what I just shared is out of character for most

professionals. Expressing emotions like grief and sorrow is

deviation from the norm for many – maybe because it's a

vulnerable act. We prefer to exhibit the cliché behavior of "faking

it 'til you make it." But this impacts educators in a unique way

because it negatively impacts an educator's ability to empathize

with his or her students. Appropriate demonstrations of emotion,

on the other hand, are profound opportunities to set examples of healthy emotional integration in the classroom. When students witness their educators' struggles, it carves out a safe place for students to struggle, too.

FAILURE

Another radical act of vulnerability is being willing to fail – and being open about it when it happens. Not only does doing so demonstrate that failure is acceptable, but it provides the opportunity for a vital lesson: teaching students how to process the difficult emotions surrounding failure and move forward from failure. Fellow educators, never be afraid to fail or make mistakes in front of your students. Seriously. Give yourself and your students permission to fail – and you'll also give yourself and your students the confidence to keep trying.

This is such a crucial value that I tell my staff every year that they have permission to fail. I encourage them to be innovative, creative, and experimental (within legal and ethical bounds!) without fear of judgment and evaluation. When teachers are willing to put themselves out there and try new things, students will follow – and the school culture will be one of innovation and growth instead of repression and fear.

Educators, this is your exhortation to try new things – to step outside of your comfort zones and make the classroom a safe space for the discomfort of tough emotions, failure, and growth. Let your students see you for who you are instead of merely your role. Doing so will open the door for connection, relationship building, and truly effective teaching.

Are you seeing the pattern in this book? Connection over conformity. Relationship over rules. Just as we can't drive our vehicles without fuel, we can't drive instruction without empathy, kindness, and love. This fuel will further our students on the road to success. It will fuel them through dark nights, fear-inducing exams, and their imperfect but important relationships. Data, curriculum, and instructional strategies are just noise if they exist outside of an environment rich in encouragement, empowerment, and empathy.

Speaking of encouragement – if you're still reading and you aren't my wife or my mother, thank you for sticking with me as I explored failing and feeling the hard things. Go refill whatever you've been sipping on through the first few chapters. When you come back, we'll discuss more specifically how educators can put their humanity into action, and how that impacts students for the better.

CHAPTER 3

Reach before Teach

If we want students to be interested in their learning, we must

first show interest in them.

TEACHING

If I was the superintendent where my old self was teaching, I'd fire me.

I'm embarrassed even writing about this, but my formative years of teaching were not my finest. My classroom management style was rules-based. I was a lecturer and a worksheet giver. If a student could memorize, they did very well in my class. The main objective I had for students was for them to perform and to conform; to take notes, do the assignments, and then do well on the test. Students were to sit in desks and speak only when called upon.

I was also self-centered and egotistical. I taught in a way that was comfortable for me, and I had little regard for the comfort of my students.

It absolutely pains me to think of how many children came through my classes who needed a connection emotionally and/or socially and I missed it. How many children reached out to me but were met with dead air and no hand to latch on to? How many students came to my classroom every day with trauma and anxiety? Rather than fostering relationships and connecting with these kids, my goal was for them to put up and shut up. I did more teaching than reaching. I'm embarrassed and ashamed of my teaching approach during those years – and as I said, had the

Travis of today supervised "new teacher Travis," I would have fired me.

A concrete example of why can be found in my second year of teaching. It was the last day of the year. I had group of students taking a final exam. One girl finished her test but still had a week-old assignment to turn in. Even though I had reminded her many times, she refused to do it.

It's worth noting this girl didn't have the greatest family life. I don't know every detail, but I knew enough to know that school was probably the place she found the most comfort. Unfortunately, I didn't take this into account. I gave her the last 15 minutes of class to do the assignment; if it wasn't completed by then, she'd receive a zero. I hate zeros today, but I didn't then – and when she didn't turn in the assignment by the time the bell rang, a zero is exactly what she got. Ultimately, the lack of points for that assignment gave her a failing grade for the class. Even half the assignment would have given her a passing grade, but I stuck to my word and I gave her a zero.

There are two major problems with that situation. The first is that I didn't care about why she didn't hand in her assignment. I was solely concerned about what she wasn't doing. The second is that the zero I gave her didn't reflect her intelligence or learning. Instead, it represented a behavior that was motivated by several outside sources.

A zero for not completing an assignment is a not a true representation of a child's acquisition of knowledge or skill; it's a punishment for behavior. Furthermore, zeroes are deflating to a student's grade and morale. By grading behaviors, we fail to steward our students' educations. By seeking to understand and appropriately respond to behaviors, we can help children grow

personally and see an improvement in grades.

Another example of a time I failed to reach occurred in

my first year as an educator. A student would often write me notes

and leave them on my desk. I got them frequently, but I often

ignored them without even looking at them.

One day after school, I walked into my second-floor

classroom. This same student was crying on the classroom

balcony. She told me she was going to jump off the ledge. After a

lengthy conversation, I persuaded her to come back inside, and I

escorted her down to the office. When I got back upstairs, I

noticed a note she'd left earlier that day.

In short, her note expressed that nobody ever noticed her.

She had no friends. Her family life wasn't good. She didn't want

to live anymore. If I knew and felt then what I know now and feel now, I could have had a more positive impact on this student's life. The same goes for the girl who refused to turn in her assignment.

I was also the head basketball coach at the first two schools where I held a teaching position, and the coach in me was no different than the teacher in me. I wanted to win. My passion for winning eclipsed my passion for the game. As with teaching, I was demanding without understanding; and if I was the athletic director back then, I would have fired myself as coach with no regrets.

As I write this, I wonder how many opportunities I missed to hear somebody's story or make someone's day brighter. When I reflect upon the zero effort I gave to show love and care for some of these kids, it's not hard to see why they sometimes gave zero academic effort. If we want students to be interested in their learning, we must first show interest in them.

REACHING

I have empathy for the mountains of pressure educators face to ensure all children are succeeding at high levels. Teachers are not held accountable for their focus on equipping students to pursue their passions – but rather for lesson plans, curriculum mapping, and high-stakes test performance. Educators spend much of their time conforming and expecting their students to do the same. They're fearful of deviating from the norm because that's what they're evaluated on. It's harmful to our students and causes teacher burnout. Educators, legislators, administrators, parents, and community members, ask yourselves this: do you get so caught up in the world of conformity and expectations that you lose sight of what truly matters?

This goes back to empathy over expectation, connection over conformity, relationship over rules. We must make relationship building a top priority in our schools. Relationships are vital to the success of any individual or organization. The original "3 Rs" of education – reading, writing, and arithmetic – cannot be scolded into students. Without reaching toward each other and building relationships (the fourth and fifth "Rs" we've always needed), information can't be successfully communicated by teachers or absorbed by students. We must cultivate daily a sense of self-worth in and appreciation for our students.

The same goes for teachers. If we want teachers to perform at high levels, we must promote their holistic wellbeing. When people are appreciated, they perform better. If I knew this when I first started teaching, connection, not conformity, would have been my goal.

OPPORTUNITIES

Believe it or not, I've had this conversation with many educators. I get this response frequently: "We do prioritize relationship building within our school." In other words, "We're fine." Unfortunately, "I'm fine" is one of the most frequent lies we tell and believe.

But let's not settle for "I'm fine" in our schools. Based on student need and the potential for human error, it's imperative to continually evaluate our relational approach and look for ways to carry it out more thoroughly and compassionately. Individual educators and school districts should evaluate and prioritize relationship building skills as rigorously and regularly as they evaluate curriculum and professional development. Unhealthy relationships render curriculum ineffective.

If you're ready to start right now, here are a few basic questions to help you check your own heart throughout the day:

- How many times do you walk by a fellow human being without saying a kind word?
- How many times do you assume others are fine because you are?
- How many times do you judge with your eyes only instead of choosing to ask questions and listen with your heart?

If we continue to downplay relationships, students and teachers will struggle to perform highly. They may comply with expectations but complying and thriving are not synonymous.

This raises another question: is compliance our standard for school culture? Is that all we want from our students and teachers? Is minimal courtesy our goal – or do we want to lavish kindness and dignity and empathetic connection upon everyone we meet?

I hope you won't settle for compliance and conformity. I hope you'll strive for connection. I hope you won't take a single smile for granted – and that you remember that there's always more going on than meets the eye. The current superintendent of Beulah Public Schools takes anxiety medication. The kid who loves volleyball struggles to get out of bed in the morning. The perky mom you saw at the supermarket was raised in domestic violence. The student who knocks on your door needs love and attention now, not tomorrow. Don't miss an opportunity to see people for who they really are. Don't miss an opportunity to hear someone's story.

CHAPTER 4

It Costs Nothing

By showering the world with positives,

we can drown out the negatives.

This is where the rubber meets the road. It's where I address the practice of prioritizing relationships and educating the heart in a system that hyper-prioritizes standards-based performance. This is where I talk about facilitating joy.

I don't have every answer, but I do know that in the Beulah school district, how you score isn't a measure of who you are. The pursuit of educational success is about equipping each student to discover their abilities and realize their dreams. We approach this process relationally because people learn better when they're respected and loved. Here are several examples of initiatives we've taken to facilitate learning in a way that celebrates our staff and students.

POSITIVE WHISTLEBLOWER CAMPAIGN

It's 1:30 am, and I'm lying next to my fourth-grade son who awoke his mom and I about a half hour ago. He had a bad dream. He dreamt that he was in the middle of a terrorist attack. Unfortunately, this is not the first time, second time, or even tenth time that I've found myself lying next to my son telling him that bad dreams are not real. But as I lay here disgusted with what the world has come to, I'm second guessing my "nightmares are not real approach."

Honestly, I'm at a loss for words. I'm a father and a school superintendent, I should have the answers for my child. I'm conflicted because good dreams, we tell kids, can be a reality. If you dream it, you can achieve it; right?

I don't want to have discussions with my children about mass shootings, bomb threats, and mass homicides by vehicles. But my child is lying next to me (asleep now), worried about things I would have never thought of when I was a kid. Honestly, my main concerns at his age was whether Santa could fit down our chimney, or what happens if the Energizer Bunny stopped "going."

What hasn't stopped though is the constant reminders on TV that we live in a world of anger. I find it sad that my child knows just about everything there is to know about Stephen Paddock. I also find it sad that I don't even have to explain who he was to you all because you are all aware. I find it disgracefully sad that the media will share his picture and life story way more than they would ever share this article.

I now live in a world in which I must explain to my children that even bad things can happen in God's house. We called that "church" growing up. We were always told to be quiet and respectful in God's house. Of course, I would pass this as advice down to my own children, but then I get the question from my child; why would somebody murder people in a church?

So now I'm lying here trying to figure out an answer for that too. Instead, I should be formulating an answer to, "why is the sky blue," or "Dad, if we dug a hole straight down could we get to China."

I can't really explain how frustrated I am. If you know me, you know that I try to infuse positivity into this world as much as I possibly can. It feels about as tough as it would be for somebody with asthma trying to get air into their lungs. Believe me, I know what it's like. When we are low on air, we take a rescue breath with our inhalers. Our airway is then clear and taking a breath doesn't hurt our chest.

Well, the world needs an inhaler right now. We need a breath of positivity. We need the media to write the positive story and to stop glorifying the negative. We cannot conquer hate with hate. We must do so with love.

I know that in just a few hours I will be back at work and over 700 students (many with similar nightmares as my child) need me to bring a smile to their face. They need to be loved. They need me to be that Energizer Bunny that keeps going and going.

My battery will run out someday. I may even die in a terrorist attack, but until that day comes I will continue to pour positivity into the hearts of people. I will continue to tell kids that the world is an amazing place, and a church is a safe place. Good will conquer evil, but we must share the good more than the evil. We must continue to bring light where there is darkness, hope where there is despair, and courage where there is fear.

My son is sound asleep now. I have tremendous hope for him. His good dreams can become a reality, and unfortunately so can his bad dreams. I'll never stop infusing positivity into him and all the other children I see daily. However, it's 2:23am now and I'd like to continue my dreams before I awake for work. I'm going to dream that positivity such as this will be shared more than Stephen Paddock's face. I'm going to dream of a media station that only writes and shows positive stories. I'm going to dream that if I decide one day to run for public office with the slogan "Make Common Sense Common Again," that I will be elected. I'm going to dream of *a better world for my kids and grandkids, and yes, if I dream it, I can achieve it."*

The above is a blog post I wrote called "Kids and Nightmares in the Aftermath of Tragedy." It was a response to the Las Vegas shooting in October 2017 – and it sparked the idea that, in a world where bad news sells, we can give sensational good news away for free. Naturally, I wanted this implemented in my school district; the kids there need it. So we started a good news campaign called the "Beulah Miner Whistle Blowers." Staff sent me the names of students and colleagues who positively impacted our school. Each day, we celebrated several individuals and shared their beautiful contributions (and their beautiful faces!) to our school's Facebook page. It sparked conversations with each of the people we celebrated – conversations not merely about their good deeds, but about life in general.

This program opened the door for celebration and connection. This project didn't cost a dime, but the return on our investment of time was invaluable. It was great watching the support, gratitude, and celebration of others fill our Facebook page and the halls of our school.

BEULAH MINERS WHISTLE BLOWERS

Blowing the whistle on positive news.

We are blowing the whistle on Carl Blackhurst. Mr. Blackhurst is the Activities Director at BPS. He spends many hours at the school making sure our activities run smoothly. On top of this is his commitment to student learning and success.

#BEULAHMINERPRIDE

#EDUZERO

In the spring of 2018, Governor Doug Burgum and the North Dakota DOT launched Vision Zero – an initiative to have zero fatalities on North Dakota roadways. I loved the concept and was inspired by his ambition, so when I was given the opportunity to speak at North Dakota's Summit on Innovative Education, I introduced an educational form of the initiative: #EduZero. The goal of this initiative is to leave zero student passions undiscovered, zero stories unheard, zero gifts unwrapped – and ultimately, have zero student suicides in the 2018-2019 school year. The school year has just begun as I'm writing this, but this is something that we should strive for every single year. There are many ways to approach this, but the bottom line is to connect *before* with your students before you correct their grammar. What that looks like in your classroom is for you to decide.

In the state of North Dakota, the need for a program like #EduZero is urgent, because the suicide rate is higher than the national average. That's why I challenged 500 educators to join me. To affect culture change across the state, we need statewide participation. The same can be said for our national culture – so I encourage you to join us, too. Share the #EduZero challenge with your colleagues. This vision shouldn't be limited to students.

If you'd like to learn more about #EduZero I encourage you to read the blog post I wrote that introduced it by visiting tjordan.org/2018/08/15/eduzero.

CHRISTMAS KINDNESS TREE

Christmas is a joyous time for many of us – a time for family gatherings, gift exchanges, feasting, and making happy memories. But that's not a universal experience. For some, Christmas is stressful – depressing, even. Many children don't receive gifts, have the luxury of quality time with family, or enjoy an abundance of food.

This is precisely why I challenge our staff and students to spread extra kindness and positivity during the holiday season. "Christmas Kindness Trees" – an idea I got from I-don't-remember-where – is how we make that happen in our school district. Here's a picture of ours, designed by my wonderful administrative assistant:

The objective is for students and staff to open an envelope and perform whatever act of kindness is inside. Once the kindness is performed, the person who did it shares a written post or a picture with a certain hashtag announcing what they did. The envelope stays with the tree and new task is put inside.

It's not rocket science. It's not magic. It's not unattainable. This is as simple as it gets. It encourages love for others and recognition of good deeds. It promotes kindness and brings smiles to faces. A smile can be all the fuel someone needs to get through the day, so it's certainly worth your time.

Steal the idea. Manipulate it and make it your own. We certainly did – and it was a hit.

OLWEAUS BULLYING PREVENTION PROGRAM

You may have this program in your schools already. This was implemented at Beulah Public Schools during the 2016-2017 school year. This happened to be my first year in the district.

Our principal at the time was Mr. Kevin Hoherz. You can find him on Twitter at @kevinhoherz. I tell you this because you're going to want to connect with him. He was instrumental in getting this program off the ground and running for us. He's filled with great ideas for promoting positive school culture. In fact, put this book down and go follow him on Twitter. I'll wait.

Now that you're back: the reason we launched this program had much to do with the data we got back from our Youth Risk Behavior Surveys (YRBS). Our school was average or above average in almost every category on the survey. We had to address it, and this program seemed to be a good fit.

In Beulah, we wanted it to be more than a bullying prevention program. Specifically, we wanted it to be a catalyst for discussion and problem-solving around the real issues our students face, so we created small groups that met twice a month. Within these groups, teachers facilitated discussions on many topics. The meetings provided our students with the confidence to speak up about issues they would normally not talk about.

Then, our teachers teamed students up for community-building projects. For example, our entire district participated in a tee shirt tie-dye event to raise awareness about bullying and allow younger students to see older students modeling exceptional behavior.

Three years later, our YRBS results have improved considerably. We still have a long way to go, but we're purposeful with this program and look for ways to improve it every year.

This program is a wonderful tool that encourages students to tell their stories. There's nothing more powerful than the stories of our students. We must do everything in our power to ensure that we cultivate environments in which our students feel comfortable telling their stories. This program certainly helps with that – and because it's so adaptable, I encourage you to research it and implement it within your own school district. And – as previously mentioned – reach out to Kevin if you need ideas.

He's as generous with innovation as he is with kindness, and he'd be happy to share some ideas with you.

IMPACT

The approximate counselor-to-student ratio in U.S. schools is 1 to 482.

Let that sink in. Every single day, students face a litany of challenges from hunger to domestic violence – and, according to the National Association for College Admission Counseling, there is one counselor for every 482 students.

Recognizing the need for more accessible counseling services, we implemented a program called IMPACT (Integrating Mental Health, Physical Health, And Coordination of Care Together). I've enlisted the help of some amazing people to help me explain this program in more detail. The next few paragraphs are contributions from Chastity Dolbec, RN, BSN, Director of

Patient Care & Innovation, and practicing physician Dr. Aaron Garman, MD – both employees of Coal Country Community Health Center (CCCHC).

As rural family practice physicians, providing the highest quality of care to our patients comes first. One change that's helped us succeed in delivering quality care is the migration of medical practice from volume-based care to value-based care. Change is always difficult, but this change was long overdue and highly beneficial for healthcare recipients.

Part of value-based care is looking for opportunities to improve. Something we keep coming back to is understanding and working with the social determinants of health. A mere 20% of a person's health is determined by the provision of care in the walls of a clinic or hospital. A full 80% is determined by social, economic, demographic and genetic factors. So how can we, a small rural clinic in the middle of nowhere, impact the lives of the patients that we serve?

First, we need to think out of the box – that is, the four walls of our clinic. We need to start thinking of healthcare as caring for the whole person, which means caring for the social determinants that comprise 80% of their health. We can't influence genetics, but we can start looking at social determinants and try to address them to the best of our ability.

Doing that for our children means going to where they are: school. That thought prompted us to start our IMPACT program. This collaboration between the local school system and the local clinic has fostered the integration of mental health providers into the school system. The next step is to increase the availability and accessibility of mental and physical health care to our students.

CCCHC and Beulah School District launched a pilot program during the 2017-2018 school year to facilitate mental health intervention for at-risk students, which included the on-going development of a sustainable framework for the provision of mental health screening and follow-up treatment plans within the four walls of the school. Additional goals of the program included universal screening through the BIMAS-2 (a brief, repeatable, multi-informant measure that can be used to identify students who might be at risk or in need of further assessment) and Progress Monitoring (assessing the effectiveness of system-wide interventions). Furthermore, the school district and CCCHC support staff attendance at the Advancing School Mental Health Conference to support growth and evidence-based expansion for the provision of mental health within the school district.

The next step in providing more accessible physical health is expanding the school staff to include a nurse practitioner. It is our hope that we can address the emotional, behavioral, and physical needs of kids in school.

In conclusion, addressing the social determinants of health requires creativity and a more widespread presence within the community. This should benefit our patients, our schools, and our communities. Ultimately, the development of healthy children into well-adjusted, well-educated adults will provide the biggest IMPACT on our healthcare system and communities.

– Chastity & Aaron

Before we move on, I want to champion and express gratitude for the entire staff at Coal Country Community Health. Not only are they committed to the holistic wellbeing of our community – but it was through them that we received a grant for a licensed school psychologist. This was huge because, unlike most other ideas in this chapter, staffing a licensed counselor is costly. For that reason, we consider ourselves fortunate to have not one but *three* school counselors that serve three separate school buildings. We're also doing what we can to further the reach of this program, because one counselor per building isn't enough to meet the increasing needs of our student population.

THERAPY DOG

Two years ago, Heather Brandt – Beulah's elementary school counselor – suggested utilizing a therapy dog to enhance our student counseling services. Here's what Heather has to say about this initiative:

I'm the handler of an amazing therapy dog named Alex. Although I'm not an expert in the area of pet therapy, Alex and I have been part of something greater than I could have imagined.

When I approached my school board about bringing in a dog to add to my school-counseling curriculum, there were many unknowns, many concerns, and many questions. Mr. Jordan understood the concerns, but his response demonstrated his undeterred commitment to Beulah's students: "Let's give it a try. If it helps just one student, it's worth it."

Alex provides some of the comfort and affection our students need to thrive. The students are willing to share more about their struggles with Alex present; he hears their stories with unwavering faithfulness and no judgement. Alex builds trust with Beulah's students as they open up about extreme sadness and extreme excitement. Without fail, smiles beam across students' faces whenever they see him.

Students have shared with me that Alex gives them an overall "feel good" sense of happiness. It can be hard to express the loving bond with Alex, but students have shared experiences such as, "Alex helped me feel calm," "I felt special when working with Alex," "Alex likes me," and "Alex taught me something about myself and how to manage my emotions."

As a school counselor, a large part of my role is to support student's social and emotional learning. One way to support development in these areas is to allow students to experience their emotions, learn coping skills to regulate the emotions when necessary, and move forward. Alex listens to students as they read, watches them as they draw, listens to and soothes them when they are not calm – and thereby contributes to their growth. Alex's role in emotional regulation skills is as big as mine when working with students. All students find comfort when petting him, talking to him, and walking with him. Their focus changes, their attitudes shift, and they leave my office with the skills and the calm to navigate their emotional battles. They leave my office provided with

unconditional love and support, and ready to learn and accomplish

the tasks of the day.

– Heather Brandt

Isn't that beautiful? Even better: Alex isn't contracted and

doesn't have due-process rights!

I kid!! The actual best part about Alex is the joy he brings

to our students every day. We could not be more honored to have

Alex on our team and we are grateful for the passion and drive

that Mrs. Brandt brought forward with this idea.

THE BOTTOM LINE

Nothing that we've done in Beulah is rocket science.

Except for the IMPACT program, everything has cost us zero

dollars. The IMPACT program is funded through a grant from

our local health care provider. I state this to clarify that while the intention of this book isn't to give you must-try ideas for your schools, one of the goals is to suggest viable possibilities for positive change in your school district. The world around us may continue talking about high stakes testing and assessments, but I'm done buying into it. Emotionally, physically, socially – and yes, academically – the pressures of standardization are costing our students as much as it costs us financially to serve them.

In order to truly serve our students, we need to put connection over conformity. Great culture and great learning go together like peanut butter and jelly. You show me a school culture teeming with excellent teachers and cared-for students, and I'll show you a classroom ripe with learning and skill acquisition.

Ok, my sandwich analogy made you hungry. Go ahead – make yourself a sandwich and come right back here. While I'm waiting for you, I'll shut off my laptop and do the same.

CHAPTER 5

Un-standardizing Standard

Sometimes our greatest learning is unlearning.

STANDARDS AREN'T SERVING US

So far, I've been privileged to discuss with you the necessity of human connection in our classrooms. I want to focus this chapter on standards and normalcy – and how those concepts are fragmenting education.

The word "standard" has two meanings in education. First, it refers to a set of skills – a benchmark that is often a goal for a child to reach. Secondly – and more detrimentally – it refers to the idea that behavior, learning capacities, and people are the same.

But . . . are they? Of course not! Yet our current educational environments are designed to treat them like they are. We fail to allow our students to learn at their own pace. We expect the same results from every single child. We're teacher-centered and practice "sit-and-get" instruction. We concern ourselves with knowledge regurgitation. We believe that the knowledge is the primary – and perhaps the only – key to success.

And that's the way it's always been done. We've deceived ourselves into thinking that because it worked for us, it should work for our kids – although we often fail to assess our own true success outside of income. We crave straight A's and high GPAs – the numbers that colleges demand. To our detriment, we've never ventured from an educational system designed for the Industrial Revolution.

But the Industrial Revolution is over. The world today

needs knowledge and resource creation. This is partly because almost every person in the world today is knowledgeable. We have information-regurgitating devices at our fingertips – and prioritize memorization anyway. The world inside our classrooms doesn't mirror the world outside our classrooms. Innovation, invention, and creation dominate our culture . . . but in the classroom we focus on standardizing and normalizing our students. There's a discrepancy between what the world needs and how we equip our students for that world.

Most people have a definition of normal – but that definition is usually limited and inconsistent with reality. For proof, I'll refer you to the diverse human experiences that have been shared with you in the first four chapters of this book. But even if you're convinced that there is a such thing as a "normal" kid, let me ask you this: if normal is the goal, how can we improve as a society? Complacency and maintaining the status quo is simply unproductive.

Breaking the status quo means understanding that differences are standard. It means celebrating differences and individuality within communities. It means creating opportunities to for students to use their gifts and talents in the classroom. In doing this, we build the framework for learning and teamwork.

Traditionally, we've forced students to fit the curriculum. The lucky students fit well and succeed – some even thrive. But many more students flounder in this sit-and-get model.

What if we allowed the talents and gifts of each student to become the curriculum? What if we molded the two together? What if we insisted that every student be allowed to use their gifts and talents in every classroom setting?

Think back to when you were a student. Were you encouraged to do what you do best every single day? Or did many of your talents go unnoticed in school because you simply didn't have the opportunity to present them?

Rather than ensuring that no child is left behind, standardization is limiting the possibilities for many children. An inability to thrive in educational settings is becoming the norm – and that should scare us. How many passions and dreams are crushed each day because we expect our students to mirror information-regurgitating smartphones instead of people? And at what point are students supposed to feel valued for who they are (not how they perform) when we don't allow ourselves to learn from them, celebrate their dreams, and support them in healthy risk taking? At what point during insistence on conformity are students expected to contribute to progress?

Fear of deviation from conformity stifles learning – but when students are allowed and encouraged to integrate their talents and gifts in the classroom, they're given the opportunity to thrive.

BRAINSTORMING PERSONALIZED LEARNING

Even if connection is our priority, conformist curriculum won't serve our students. We need to find a manageable, personalized approach to education. Knowing this, a group of educators and other professionals (including myself) have started brainstorming a personalized, competency-based approach to graduation.

Many high school juniors and seniors are taking classes they won't use later in life; the "why do I need this" question reveals this reality all too well. Sometimes we can justify our broad and standardized curriculum; often, especially in the later years, we can't. I myself have yet to use the square-root of four in my job. I haven't needed to reference the periodic table, either. But if I'd been allowed to intern as a senior, my career could have been fast-tracked – and many students can say the same. My brainstorming group discussed internship-focused senior years for that reason. Students could experiment with different fields so that they have a clearer idea of what college major to choose. They could even earn money and save for college, all the while acquiring and demonstrating mastery of skills that would make them more eligible candidates for today's competitive workforce.

I'm excited to see what else we come up with – and I'm excited to hear from the readers of this book. What ideas do you have for personalized, competency-based education? Tweet them to me at @supt_jordan!

TIME CAN BE ON OUR SIDE

Academic standards aren't the only detrimental standards in the educational system. Standard time constraints are problematic, too. Currently, in education, time is a constant and learning is a variable. What this means is that time is prioritized over learning. Our classes are divided into minutes, our years into semesters, our semesters into quarters – and within those constraints, due dates are attached to all classwork. Time partially dictates whether learning occurred or didn't occur – and instead of grading solely on learning, competency, or even the ability to meet a standard, we end up grading a child's ability to meet a deadline. Instead of reaching to students in their need, we teach them to conform to our timetables.

You already know that I've been there and done that as an educator. It embarrasses me to admit this, but I actually gave

77

assignments to fill time and then docked points when assignment completion exceeded the time I was trying to fill!

If this is where you currently are in education, don't get down on yourself. Life isn't just about where you are currently; it's about where you are going. And this is an opportunity to unlearn conformity and relearn – or learn for the first time – true subject matter education. (By the way, *The Unlearning Leader* by Michael Lubelfeld and Nick Polyak is a great book to help you through that process. The guys who wrote it are education rock stars.)

No matter how much time it takes, learning should be the constant. Meeting students where they are and allowing them to learn at a pace which makes sense for their development will better equip them for this world than perpetually grading behavior. We turn too many children away from school because they don't meet deadlines. A child has trouble handing in work on time (for reasons that are often out of his/her control); as a result, his or her grades begin to plummet. Eventually they fall so far behind that they no longer see a way to catch up – and they drop out.

When I question educators about this, I almost always get the same response: "How can we teach our students to be responsible if we don't give them deadlines?"

You've heard it too, haven't you? Maybe you even agree with it. Let me tell you, there are thousands of ways to teach responsibility without attaching grades and deadlines. Start with yourself as an educator. Model responsibility. Positively reinforce responsible behavior. Have high expectations for your students and praise them when they exhibit responsibility. Be willing to look for and attempt to meet your students' needs for additional time, repetition, and instruction. Be aware that their world outside of school may be complete chaos. They may spend the hours away from school exhibiting responsibility beyond assignment completion by taking care of a sibling, taking care of their parents, or working a job to help family finances. They may not have the resources at home to do the work required. Maybe they don't even have a home.

Personally, I'd have neither a driver's license nor an educator's license if my learning was constrained to a timeline. It took me two times to pass my driving test – and let's just say that the Praxis was much harder than I thought it would be. But choosing to pursue what I wanted and needed to thrive, even after failure, was a greater display of responsibility than succeeding on somebody else's timeline. All students need that lesson on perseverance and taking ownership of their learning more than they need a lesson on taking ownership of their educators'

timelines.

CHAPTER 6

When Politics Disrupt Education

Education should not be influenced by politics; rather, politics should be influenced by education.

Throughout the course of this book, I've outlined several opportunities for progress. Many are doable in every school district and on every budget – but revising curriculum and providing better healthcare requires outside help. To affect dramatic, lasting change in our educational system, we have to tap into everything that influences it. That includes (groan) politics. This isn't a book on legal education policy, so I'm only going to devote one chapter to my thoughts on this subject.

I have a personal stake in the success of students, educators, administrators, and the educational system as a whole.

Mind, body, and soul, I've dedicated my life to this cause. My investment includes countless hours of training and prep in my post-secondary and master's programs; it includes the many years I've spent within the walls of schools. Throughout my lifelong commitment, I've watched decisions and agendas from our nation's highest levels get pushed into schools. Frankly, I struggle to fully affirm the role politics plays in education, and I struggle to understand the direction it's taking us.

One political pain-point for me pertains to the gun control debate. We experience tragedy at the hands of broken people, and rather than ramping up our efforts to arm students with hope, we fight amongst ourselves and attempt to pass legislation about arming school staff. Grief and loss are preyed upon to further political agendas while student and community needs for hope and love remain unmet. How many people are isolated with nothing but bad news for company while the rest of the world takes sides? While we adhere to our political party affiliations, we disregard the undebatable value of every human being and an ages-old, life-affirming call to action: love your neighbors. It's no wonder our schools remain broken.

Another example of political hindrance is School Choice, a federal initiative that allows a family to take their kids from one school and enroll them in another. This program was supposedly designed with families in mind, but it's had a negative impact on our nation's education system. Understandably, some parents want their children to thrive – and if the move turns out to be a positive thing for a struggling child, that's great for that child and that family. But that's not a viable option for every family, so School Choice creates a system of haves and have nots. Some kids get to move and grow; others don't. Instead of solving the school's problems to provide greater stability and improved wellbeing for *all* students, we allow the privileged freedom to move and ignore the problems facing the students who remain.

School Choice advocates will tell you that the school will have no choice but to get better or they'll lose their students – but again, not all families can move their kids around. In a system such as this we further divide our students and schools. In a few words, we need our policy makers to trust teachers, address student needs holistically, and offer less regulation and more service.

Sometimes I feel a campaign coming in my future with the slogan "Make Common Sense Common Again" – but more than education needs the influence of well-meaning politicians, politicians need the influence of our educational systems as they are and as they could be.

In many ways, that starts with trusting and equipping educators. I'm grateful for the support we *do* have from the government – but nobody is more knowledgeable about the needs of our students than the teachers and administrators who serve them daily. For that reason, funding needs to be reassessed – as does our system of evaluating educators based on standardized test scores. Like students, every teacher has specific needs; regular, two-way communication and evaluation would allow schools to build more effective support systems for teachers.

Boiled down even further, this is about maintaining a proper focus. When decisions are implemented with deference to political affiliation, special interests, and hitting government-issued numbers and/or proficiencies, children and teachers get left behind. In fact, there isn't a single law, measure, or act that ensures children will learn; but studies do demonstrate that safe, nurturing environments increase a student's capacity to learn. For

students to thrive on their educational journeys, policy must

focus on holistic wellbeing, celebration of individuality, and

curriculum that incorporates and makes room for students'

passions. Education policy makers, like teachers, should be on

mission to ensure students know they matter. This will encourage

student attendance and engagement, which is a great step toward

achieving at high levels.

I need to be clear: this is not about providing blanket fixes

from the top. No such thing can address the needs of all schools.

Rather, it's about providing schools with the resources and the

freedom to meet their varying needs. Under-achieving schools

can't be improved with standardized approaches any more than

under-achieving students can be served with standardized

curriculum. Positive and impactful change will not result from rigid policy. It will result from engaging in conversation and making relationship-building a priority. It will result from using a systematic approach to our observation and evaluation tools. This allows for both empathy and accountability to mold our schools and our students in the healthiest and most effective way.

CHAPTER 7

An Invitation to All Teachers

What's comfortable for you may not be best for your students.

I've come a long way in the fourteen years I've been involved in education. Of course, if I could go back and do it all over again, I would certainly do it differently. In my early years as an educator, my goal was to get by. I was caught up in classroom management chaos, typing notes until about 2:00 am every single day. I felt like I was Tom Hanks in Castaway – isolated on a deserted island. The only difference? He had Wilson.

"Just get by" might be a common motto at the start of a teaching career – but let me suggest a more life-giving route. Even though education is changing at a rapid pace, I invite you to remember what remains the same – because doing so will help you throughout your entire career. Pour yourself some coffee, and

let the following constants sink into your soul.

> When you come to school tired, remember that you probably have one or two students that came to school with no sleep. We have no clue what the home environment looks like for many of our students.

When you get frustrated because a child didn't turn in his or her work, remember that they may've spent the night caring for a sibling because their guardian(s) spent the night working or partying. We're also clueless about the roles our students play in their home environments.

> Remember that the home environments of any one of your students – including those attempting to fulfill parental roles – may be a car, a hotel room, or the street.

When you find it hard to get out of bed to come to work, remember that a child may wake up excited to come to school because it's the only place he or she feels safe.

> When you want to raise your voice, throw something, or bang a yardstick against a trashcan because students are acting out, remember that some students come to school to escape violence – and no student comes to school to experience it.

When you get upset because a child scored poorly on an assessment, remember that the assessment does not define the potential of that child. This is noted throughout this book. Single moments – and especially single test scores – do not define your students.

Remember that individual chapters don't communicate the entire message of a book any more than individual moments or seasons tell a person's who story. When we judge people by the chapter we walk in on, we label them (good/bad, poor/rich, smart/unintelligent, etc.) – and then we design their education around those labels. The most effective way to approach education, however, is to connect, seek to become acquainted with each child's whole story, help kids discover their passions, and structure their education around those passions.

Remember the second chances you've received throughout your life. Remember that your students deserve those as well – especially considering varying learning abilities and roles and environments that are out of your students' control.

Remember that your smile can change a moment, a day, and even a life. Smile often.

Remember that every single child is battling something – and you may be the one to help them overcome it. When a child reaches out to you, listen. If a child wants to chat with you, make it your priority to accommodate them. Grading papers can wait. Your prep time is not as important as a conversation with a child.

Make time to connect with your colleagues as well; they're usually fighting the same battles you are and watching the same students struggle.

Praise students every day. They don't all need a participation ribbon; they do need affirmation as human beings. Make it a priority to recognize that great things your students do on a daily basis.

Remember that every child has a gift that's worthy of being unwrapped. Help your students discover that gift. Facilitate the joy of unwrapping it. And celebrate the gift and unwrapping process with them.

Remember that your students are watching your every move. They will model your behavior. Always teach as if their parents are in the room.

Your role may be teaching, but who you are is a human being. Operate as a human being within your role.

Aim for exploration, risk-taking, and connection over conformity.

Thank you for accepting my invitation to read these hard truths. At worst, the reminders may have made you uncomfortable. But what's comfortable for you may not be best for your students. Don't get into the habit of teaching in a way that is easy and comfortable for you. This is the epitome of teacher-centered instruction. Your classroom should be completely student-centered and driven. You are there as a guide. Your sense of discomfort in the classroom may spark a child out of their comfort zone. It's here where true potential is realized. In my formative years as a teacher, I was consumed with content, time management, and just getting by. While I was getting by, opportunities to help children were passing by. I realize now that connections must come before curriculum. Relationships must come before reading, writing, and arithmetic. To ensure that every child learns at high levels, we must love every child at high levels. Our students deserve our very best – even if we are at our very worst.

CHAPTER 8

A Message to All Students

You are one of one. No one in the world is exactly like you are.

No one!

In my years in education, I've witnessed triumph and tragedy. I've experienced the euphoria of game-winning buzzer-beaters – and I've felt the emptiness that accompanies student depression, and in some cases, death. In the blink of an eye, the moments where everything is going right are turned upside down. You feel the pressure from the world around you. Expectations are showered upon you by parents, teachers, friends, and society in general. You try to put up an umbrella, but ultimately, it's just too much. That rain persistently erodes your individual sense of purpose and identity while you work tirelessly to fit into a mold of a demanding world's making.

Some of you do it better than others. Some of you are popular, and have a loving, supportive family at home. You have a security net to catch you when you fall, pick you up, and dust you off in times of trouble. Others of you would love to be considered popular. Your security net is weak or nonexistent. Maybe you feel alone at school, but it's the one place where you feel safe and can always get a meal. The reality is that your worlds are different, although you might never know it when you look at each other.

As you navigate this web of worlds, wondering how yours fits in with all the others, remember that you're here for a reason – and that reason isn't necessarily to "fit the mold." You were created to contribute. Author and podcaster Stephanie May Wilson put it this way:

"There is room for you. God's economy is never an economy of lack. Scarcity is not a thing in God's economy. If he has called two people to do something, even if they're similar, he has a purpose for both of those. Those things are not wasted. [. . .] Is there too much beauty in the world? No. Is there too much goodness in the world? No. Does everyone know Jesus and how much he loves them? No. Does everyone know how worthy of love [they are] and how much they're worth? No. There is not too much of that, and so until there is too much of that, or goodness in the world, the market is not saturated. We have work to do. All of us have work to do in the world. And if there are two people or a thousand people working alongside you, so much the better."

Isn't that profound? You are uniquely you. You don't have to conform to the mold, and you don't have to compare yourself, either. You are entitled to be you and are valuable just as you are.

I've visited with many students who have reached a point where they no longer want to exist. I've heard their stories and listened to their hardships. Some of these students tried to end their lives. Others ultimately did end their lives.

So, let me tell you: YOU MATTER. At your highest and your lowest, you matter. If your lives were worth giving, they are certainly worth living. I challenge all of you to stop trying to fit the mold, and instead mold yourselves into the awesome person you were meant to be. You may not know it, but you mean the world to many people. People you don't even know exist look up to you. Walk the hallways with confidence and help others do the same. You will find that by helping others (even if you need it more) you will ultimately help yourself.

When life gets you to your lowest point, find your talent and live out your passion. Every single one of you has a passion. Don't ignore it, no matter what it is. Pour your heart and soul into it. Throw your worries away and dive into you. Dive into your passion. My passion was basketball and even though I'm not playing for the Chicago Bulls right now, it has led me to be the person I am today. The passion you pursue today will help create your life tomorrow. You have the gifts to make the world a better place. Take some time to celebrate you even if you are the only one that shows up to the party.

Your life will be filled with triumphs and tribulations. You may never hit a buzzer-beater to win a game, but life is your game to win. Just remember that you are one of one and you have been

given the gifts to do just that.

CHAPTER 9

Final Thoughts

You can't be sensational without being relational.

I hope this book has successfully imparted the conviction that while teachers and students may comply with standards, they cannot sustain performance or learning at high levels when they're fighting trauma. I hope this book has instilled in you a desire to see others thrive, not just comply. I hope that as you're reading this final chapter, you're looking at education through a more relational lens. In closing, I want to leave you with a few encouraging ways to be relational, sensational, and place connection over conformity.

Be a friend. Like me, you probably fill many roles – teacher, student, husband, father, etc. As you function in those roles, offer genuine friendship to those you encounter – because friendship can provide motivation and demonstrate love. Don't forget that children need to enjoy the fruit of friendship to succeed in their roles as students.

> Value and attend to people more than their behaviors. Hurt people hurt people, and the "what" (the wounding behavior) can't be fixed if we don't understand the "why" or the "who."

Use your mouth as an agent of healing instead of a weapon. Words pushed Cassidy and others like her over the edge, so choose yours wisely.

> Don't define people by one moment, one flaw, one mistake, or one characteristic. Instead, seek to understand everyone holistically – and when you're tempted to focus on the flaws you see, work even harder to find the good.

To foster joy in relationships, remember Theodore Roosevelt's words: "Comparison is the thief of joy."

> Practice gratitude by writing down the names of the people (and things) in your life that you take for granted.

> Lastly, I want to leave you with the very same Zig Ziglar

quote I started this book off with:

A lot of people have gone further than they thought they could

because somebody else thought they could.

One of the greatest gifts we can give someone else is the gift of belief. Sometimes a little push or encouragement from someone else can help somebody find their passion and begin to live it. The reward for believing in someone is immeasurable. It's a gift that keeps giving – because just as hurt people hurt people, inspired people inspire people.

Imagine every human being in the world being loved and inspired. How awesome would that be?

ABOUT THE AUTHOR

I'm just a guy with a passion. A passion to change the world. I believe we can do better as educators, parents, business leaders, politicians, media specialists, and all other roles. I've spent my entire life in the world of education. My experiences as a student were not so great. My first years as a teacher were consumed with just getting by and conforming to the norms. I hated writing when I was a student and I hated speaking. Now I've written a book and started a side gig as a motivational speaker. I'm a status quo shaker, a conformity breaker, and a difference maker. Feel free to connect with me about this book, a speaking event, or the world of education.

With Love,
Travis Jordan

Twitter	@supt_jordan
Email	inspiringsupt@gmail.com
Blog	tjordan.org

BIBLIOGRAPHY

Jordan, Travis. "#EDUZERO." *Beyond Measure*, 15 Aug. 2018, tjordan.org/2018/08/15/eduzero/.

Jordan, Travis. "I Cried." *Beyond Measure*, 20 Dec. 2018, tjordan.org/2018/12/20/i-cried/.

Jordan, Travis. "Kids and Nightmares in the Aftermath of Tragedy." *Beyond Measure*, 22 Nov. 2017, tjordan.org/2017/11/22/kids-and-nightmares-in-the-aftermath-of tragedy/.

"Separation anxiety disorder." *Mayo Clinic*, www.mayoclinic .org/ diseases-conditions/ separation-anxiety-disorder/ symptoms-causes/syc-20377455.

"State-by-State Student-to-Counselor Ratio Report." *National Association for College Admission Counseling*, American School Counselor Association and National Association for College Admission Counseling, www.nacacnet.org/ globalassets/ documents/publications/research/state-by-state-ratio-report.pdf.

Wilson, Stephanie May. "How to Keep Comparison from Stealing Your Joy." Stephanie May Wilson. stephaniemaywilson.com/2017/10/02/girls-night-5-how-to-keep-comparison-from-stealing-your-joy/. 2 Oct. 2017.

ACKNOWELDGEMENTS

Chastity Dolbec and Aaron Garman, thank you for contributing a statement about the history behind and function of Beulah's IMPACT program. Your commitment to Beulah's students is extraordinary.

Heather Brandt, thank you for contributing a statement about the history behind and function of utilizing a therapy animal in Beulah Public Schools. Your passion and love for Beulah's students changes lives every day.

"Mandy" and "Zoey," thank you for allowing me to share your stories with the readers of this book. May your bravery inspire others to share their own stories.

Justine Petersen, thank you for helping me articulate my message. I appreciate the work you put in to edit my words, format and style the content, and design the cover. Justine can be reached at justine.elice@outlook.com for help with your creative project.

Thank you to the amazing women and men who endorsed my book and believed in me. Your individual impacts on the world of education will be felt for generations, and I appreciate what you've done to help me make an impact of my own.

Made in the USA
San Bernardino, CA
15 July 2019